The EYES NEVER CHANGE

A Simple Woman's Journey from Madness
to Love and Compassion by Finding God

MARY ESTHER CHRISTIAN

WestBow Press books may be ordered through booksellers or by contacting:

WestBow Press
A Division of Thomas Nelson & Zondervan
1663 Liberty Drive
Bloomington, IN 47403
www.westbowpress.com
1 (866) 928-1240

Because of the dynamic nature of the Internet, any web addresses or links contained in this book may have changed since publication and may no longer be valid. The views expressed in this work are solely those of the author and do not necessarily reflect the views of the publisher, and the publisher hereby disclaims any responsibility for them.

Any people depicted in stock imagery provided by Thinkstock are models, and such images are being used for illustrative purposes only.
Certain stock imagery © Thinkstock.

ISBN: 978-1-5127-1131-8 (sc)
ISBN: 978-1-5127-1132-5 (e)

Library of Congress Control Number: 2015914466

Print information available on the last page.

WestBow Press rev. date: 10/12/2015

WESTBOW
P R E S S®
A DIVISION OF THOMAS NELSON
& ZONDERVAN

Just a reminder: The content of some of the information in these journals are of the author's own perception of reality and do not represent everyone else's perceptions.

JOURNAL ONE

Two entries were made before the first hospitalization. It took at least one year before
I was capable of forming complete thoughts. The heavily sedating medications and
cycling episodes along with caring for a four year old boy and baby girl proved
to be all I could manage. My promising future as a graphic artist/illustrator would
be over along with being a substantial financial contributor in my marriage.

March 15, 1992

There is something about Sundays. They seem to be the lazy day of the week. It is a March day, cold and colorless, yet the sun rushes through my windows and warms the rooms and hallways of my house. My little boy sleeps in the room next to me while my other child remains restless inside of me, poking and rolling. The sensation feels like bubbles bursting in my abdomen.

April 14, 1992

I have come to a conclusion. Everything in life should be a struggle. It's the only way all that is good in the world can be appreciated. And when what you have is taking away, this lesson is learned the hard way. We get so caught up in trying to control our lives and have them run smoothly, without any detours. We must learn to accept the unplanned obstacles, as difficult as they may be. Every day I can find truth in all that is around me, a child playing in a sandbox, the sounds and smells of nature in the spring time. It's all right here. I am fortunate to have this.

February 25, 1993

Nearly a year has passed since my last journal. So much has happened. My neighbor lost her husband, I had my second child, and I ended up in a psychiatric hospital. Spring will be here soon and I'm praying I will be well. Never in my entire life have I felt so alone. I'm home with my two children and my rushing thoughts, thoughts and feelings I have absolutely no control over. I feel isolated from everyone because no one knows what this is like. I'm captive, imprisoned, and frightened. Sometime's there's no safety anywhere. I could always talk myself out of a lot of things but this is different. My inner strength is no match for this turmoil inside. It's a turmoil that churns and stirs up every negative emotion possible. It eats at my soul and I long for peaceful days in my garden arranging my plants. I can't find peace anywhere. Simple things always made me happy. I found enjoyment in the small goals I set for myself. That is all vanished, my head pounds and so does my heart. At least God has given me the strength to love and take care of my children. I hope I will sleep well tonight.

February 26, 1993

Early this morning the baby woke. It was about 3:00 am. She had been teething hard that day. As I held her the thoughts began. My body began to shake. I looked in on my husband sleeping. He looked so placid, like nothing was worrying him. He slept well. Meanwhile, I was in a serious state. The anger began to swell stronger and stronger as I watched him sleep soundly. I had visions of him with whores, getting from them what he couldn't get from me. I kept thinking that no matter how much I gave, that these strong desires could only be quenched with these women. I have a vivid imagination unfortunately. The more I gave the more I found how much I needed him. The visions rushed through my head like a movie. Smugly he would joke about how good the woman he had the day before was. She was all their favorite. I had to wake him to confront him. He awoke and the arguing began, me accusing and him denying, a familiar scene except this time I pushed it too far saying things to cut him down as much as possible. I could not take these words back. He didn't even attack me back. I wanted him to. After we had quieted down I felt in a daze, a strange calm feeling. He was quiet also. I couldn't believe what I had said to him. He'll never believe I didn't mean one word. Those words were my only defense. Yet, before he left for work, he still touched me and said I love you. That's when it really hit me. No one loves me like he does, no one, not even my own mother. I was tearing him apart, trying to make him out to be the sick one, when in fact I was the one with the illness. By afternoon my emotions of hate turned to love. I began thinking about him, how good it felt to be held by him, to smell him, to love him. Can he ever forgive me? Have I gone too far? I'm destroying the love we have. This has to stop.

October 23, 1993

Death of Innocence

Walking through the woods

Trying to find my place

I know now.

I cry like the wolf

I am the prey

I pray and bow my head

I cannot turn back

With shattered ideals I walk slowly,

Carefully, not to make a sound

I want to scream

Will anybody here me

Probably just the wolves

This is the truth I cannot bare

It's too obscene this conscious

State of innocence,

This death of innocence

I just want to be held like

A child, don't abandon me

Let me weep in your arms

Until I fall asleep

Rock me slowly back and forth

Amen.

October 24, 1993

Should we give this poem

To all our daughters

For this battle can never be won

I watch my child run and play

The smile on her face is real,

The laughter is pure, like fresh

Running water,

Pure like the sun, the trees,

The earth

The universe is tucked

In her little coat pocket

October 26, 1993

Into the night with the smell of leaves decaying,

Up on a knoll, an old house

Stands, its paint peeling, its shutters fallen off,

It seems deserted.

And I look up at this hauntingly mansion and find it is being

Occupied

The shades are pulled down and the glowing blue light glows

Behind them

There are no silhouettes.

I'm hoping to see them.

I go very quietly.

October 31, 1993

Masquerade

We walk around with masquerades
Silently, cautiously, we hide
Behind the truth,
For the truth is hard to face
So we cover our faces and our hearts
Cover them so no one can see in
Keep your eyes closed
Keep them closed tightly
Put on your masquerade
Justify as much as you can but the
Masquerade cannot save you
You will never be saved
You're behind bars for the rest of
Your life
And all the laughing will not
Set you free
The Brotherhood of Men

January 9, 1994

Annie plays on the floor, amusing herself quietly. She's such a happy little soul. Very active though, she keeps me moving. We went sled riding today. It was nice except for the wind. It goes right through you. Already I'm looking forward to spring. Maybe I'd like it better if I were a skier. Right now I'm waiting for Richard to get back from plowing his Mom's driveway. It's funny, I'm home all day and I can't wait for Richard to pull in the yard. I still get that feeling I used to feel when we were going out. Over the years we weren't in touch with each other. Now it's like we rediscovered ourselves and our marriage.

March 2, 1996

I'm finally ready to make the journey. All my life I have had questions and ideas but it wasn't until my science and spirituality were thrown into turmoil that I really had to find some answers. There are many more before me that have discovered their paths. I need to discover mine, for my sake and the sake of my family. My only fear is that the chemistry of my thoughts will make me sick again. I have to take this in stride. I have to learn how to breathe the rhythm of life.

March 6, 1996

Two things happened to me today that made a strong impact. I was in the grocery store when all of a sudden this woman at the checkout counter went off. She started yelling about the way they were packing her bags. She was completely out of control. As she was walking out the door someone yelled, "Hey lady, you forgot to take your lithium." Everyone at the checkout laughed. They kept laughing and joking. This really struck a nerve. I couldn't concentrate on my shopping because I kept envisioning myself going up there and telling everybody how ignorant they were. If they only knew the suffering they wouldn't laugh. In fact, you'd never hear someone say- "Hey lady, you forgot to do your chemotherapy today."

I also went to a lecture today. Lori Schiller was the speaker. Her story was incredible. She had schizophrenia. For nine years she was in and out of hospitals. Finally, she tried a new medication and she saw results in three weeks.

I had only experienced a glimpse of this woman's torment and I felt a connection.

March 12, 1996

Well that was a short-lived journey. I thought I was on to something. I read the book 'Quantum Healing' and I thought I had all the answers or at least on the brink. My enthusiasm was a mask, for I was heading into a manic episode. I cried at the Doctor's today because all I was doing was just thinking, that's all, just thinking. I can't even think. It makes me sick. I almost didn't catch it either. I was sure my enthusiasm for this new found knowledge was just exactly that. God, this illness makes me angry!!!!

March 20, 1996

2:30 am

Receive information through senses + thought (interpretation) + response (emotion/chemicals misfiring) + more thought + response + thoughts + etc.

My interpretations make me sick and I need medication to keep symptoms under control. I need to find out why my interpretations cause imbalance.

After seeing the Doctor:

Triggers:

Sex

Birthday

Family denial

Lack of accomplishments with work

Weight

Things to do:

Think outwardly

Don't internalize

July 11, 1997

Well, well another year has gone by. I've been very well. The episodes I've had have been caught early enough and kept under control. I feel I need to write because this particular episode has a hold on me. My hand is shaking. I've gotten so good at hiding this illness. No one has a clue. Sometimes I don't even tell Richard. I don't want to be a burden. It's like being a tiger in a cage pacing back and forth one thousand times looking for a way to escape. It's like you're existing in two ways. One minute your head is about ready to explode and the next minute you're at a picnic, nodding your head and pleasantly smiling.

October 13, 1997

It has been a week and a half of delusions and hallucinations. The TV is giving me messages. Everything said and done around me feeds my delusion. I've been working up to this point for three months. I should have listened to my last entry but this time I thought I could fight it because I had been doing so well....... blah, blah, blah.

There were no entries between 1998 through 2003

November 17, 2004

A Letter to my Sister,

It's so hard to watch you suffer. You don't deserve this. You are a good person. You shouldn't have to feel this. You want answers, you just want answers. You cannot turn off your feelings. You love him. He's been your lover and friend and now he's gone, with no explanation. But it is nothing that you did. He does not know how to cope with all his problems so he's bottled them up and turned on you. I wish I had comforting words of wisdom, but I don't. I hope your therapist can help you deal with the pain. If I can be there for you I will. You are my family. I love you.

I can't help but start thinking inwardly about my painful experiences. I am not feeling sorry for myself but I can sometimes see myself in my sister, the confusion, the completely broken spirit, the inevitable surrender, the reality, the acceptance, the struggle, and the continuous attempts to cope. She is dealing with the loss of a loved one. I dealt with the loss of myself. There are some similarities. Now, for the resentment: I hate the doctor. She should have made her diagnosis and then had me go to a therapist. But instead, for years she kept medicating and medicating, in her cold medical way, without telling me to discuss my feelings with a professional therapist. So for years I had to take drugs to prevent from going insane with absolutely no answers. She is a terrible doctor and if I ever saw her I would tell her so.

November 2004

For the past four to six months I have had a higher sense of well being. I lost weight, not drastically but in a good way. I do the business bookkeeping, I work part- time, when I do projects I complete them. I do not have rushing thoughts. Richard does say he thinks I'm on the edge. But I'm functioning well. I wonder if the illness has taken on a new face and because I haven't gone delusional I think I'm ok. Has it disguised itself?

Right now I'm thinking too inwardly. But I need to write this down. I don't want to accuse and look for excuses for my problems. These are the questions:

1. Why have I always felt uncomfortable with my father having any physical contact with me? (Hugging)

2. Why for most of my life I felt uncomfortable with my sexuality? I felt it was a weakness and a submission. For the past several months it's been wonderful and free. Not hypersexual with hidden motives.

3. Why do I have an uncomfortable relationship with my brother?

4. Why did the same delusion of Richard betraying me sexually, the good and the evil, with me caught in the middle, repeat itself over and over again? Why have I been tormented by the sex and betrayal of the one man that truly loves me unconditionally? Is a repeated delusion coming from your subconscious like a bad dream? And is there some truth in it. I will answer that, because if it were so, with all the doctors and therapists I have seen, you would think they would recognize this and pursue things further. Or is it self-discovery.......
when you're finally strong enough?

November 2004

Now, for the most important questions: How have I hurt my children?

Adam:

I did not give him as much attention as I did with Annie because he did not seem to need it. He once said I like girls better than boys. He's my boy but I make a conscious effort not to give him bad feelings when I kiss him goodbye. I don't want him to feel uncomfortable. He's very sensitive. I may have giving more attention to Annie because I felt I had to protect her. In the past year Adam and I talk and laugh more. He appears to be a very stable, mature 16- year old. I'm very proud of him. There's also this special bond for me because he was breech and it was a very long and difficult birth. We got through it together.

When he was two he fractured his femur. He was in traction for one week and in a body cast for eight weeks. When he was in traction he was in agonizing pain because his leg would spasm and come flying back each time he'd try to fall asleep. When this would happen he would scream out in pain. Every time he would start to get sleepy I would brace him. But it did not help. I told God to give me the pain. And then I begged the nurses to do something. Finally, they did.

Annie:

I see parts of myself in her. She looks like me. She's creative, marches to the beat of a different drummer, misunderstood, emotional, and smart. She's loud and bossy, though. Adam once said we kiss too much. I believe I physically abused her one night. When she was grounded, I screamed at her, through her back and forth, then grabbed her and brought her upstairs. I think I threw her down on the bed and screamed at her again. I'm sure this had a profound effect on her. She has a nervous stomach. I took her to the doctor. She feels anxious when we go places. I know how she feels. When I was in first grade I missed a lot of school because I nearly had an ulcer. I had to go for a GI series and take a lot of medication. My mother told me it was the influence of the teacher.

December 26, 2004

I'm saddened this Christmas and there are tears in my eyes as I write this. I've been looking at things lately for what they truly are, my family, your family, myself, and you and me. This Christmas I was so excited to give you things from the heart. I gave you the painting because I honestly thought it meant something to you because it hung in your parent's house. I spent hours on the photos of the kids because you had mentioned how much that would mean to you. The TV was something I knew you wanted but I think it meant more to you than the photos because you never took me aside, looked at me, and said, "Thank-you so much for this, I know how much time and effort this took." Instead, you made me feel guilty for leaving early Christmas Eve. My brother gave me a book on Picasso because he knew how much I would truly appreciate it and love the artwork. If you don't know what I would like and what I would honestly enjoy, ask people that know me in that way. Do you really think a tool box is meaningful to me? I don't want material things. I want things that are who I am. One Christmas you had the kids buy me decorations that I really didn't like. If you wanted them to give me something I would like you should have gone to a special shop that sold Victorian decorations. Why do you love me? Is it for some ideals that you think love should be. And why do I love you? Is it because you love me more than anyone ever has and I needed that for my self-worth. Or do I love you for who you are and for understanding me and who I really am. Maybe it's time we talk honestly. Not surface stuff.

May 5, 2005

For weeks, at all different times of the day, early morning to dusk... the light touches many different objects in the house, the walls and through the glass. So many things are caught for just a short time so I look at the clock to see what time the light has hit these things. I wish I could capture all these instances. They're interesting. And when I drive through town I'm always looking at the different tones and hues everywhere. I'm really trying to prioritize. I have to make my kids come first. It's so hard, I'm always distracted. If I turn away and not think it's easier to focus. The more I practice this maybe I'll master it.... ignoring color, light, music. Blind and deaf but focused on one thing, doing things for Richard and the kid's, the business, home. Lists help. I get very tired, inside and out. It seems my mind never stops or I have lapses when I stare into space, resting..... in and out, but mostly in. When I rest I don't think clearly, things do not register. But that's only for a short while. When I come back, the shutter speed snaps quickly, trying to take it all in - efficiently, through my eyes and ears. It's nearly impossible to turn away.

November 12, 2005

This past year has been my best year and my most frustrating. There is a lot of suffering in this world.... young children, young mothers, old people. And some people make themselves miserable. I'm one of those. I have so much anger and resentment. There is something very deeply wrong with me. I can't fight the fact that I'm wired wrong. I thought I had come out on the other side. I don't think I have. I'm spiraling and now the question is, "What is the best thing to do for the kids?" I distract myself by obsessing with projects to find fulfillment. I love the kids, taking care of a home....simple things. But I have beaten Richard down and he's finally tired. So am I. Sometimes people should just go away. Adam will be ok, he's a boy. He will have Richard... but Annie, I have to really make sure she'll be in good hands with a woman who will understand her. If she has this I know she'll be ok. Richard's eyes have been opened. I will never change.

Behind white picket fences there are tortured souls.

JOURNAL TWO

In 2006 my doctor took me off a medication because he felt I would manage on just one of the medications. He said that bi-polar II patients had success with this type of management...I was bi-polar I.

It was the middle of the night when I reached crisis level. I woke up and saw the moonlight coming through the skylight. I got out of bed and knelt down in the rays of light. I thought God was coming for me. I believed I was going on to the next life so I relieved myself. Once I realized I wasn't going on to the next life I began reciting the Act of Contrition. Intermittently I would lie on the floor pounding my fists in the air. I was accepting my fate of being buried alive and was pounding my way out of the coffin. Then I would get up again and with hands folded repeat the prayer. Richard woke up. He didn't know what to do. He was able to get me down stairs and into the garage. The cement felt cold on my back. I was barefoot and my nightgown was wet. He managed to get me in the truck and drove me to the ER. I remember as we pulled up to the building my heart sunk. I was about to face Hades completely alone.

The wait in the ER was long but once I got a room, Richard left and I went up on the floor. Again I began pounding my fists in the air. One of the nurses said, "Get up off the floor, you're embarrassing yourself." Then I began to crawl towards the door. It seemed 20 ft. tall. I had regressed back into a child, crying as I crawled. By now security had been called and I was being manhandled by several guards. They were bringing me into an isolation room. I screamed so loud my ears hurt. Once in the room I was forced on a bare mattress. I squirmed and fought with every ounce of strength that I had. I was being held down against my will. Then somebody pulled down the back of my pants and gave me a shot. Slowly I stopped fighting back. I could feel my legs and arms turn to rubber. The firm grips of the guards hands began to loosen. With my mouth opened, I surrendered like a dying animal.

2006

A couple days later I remember sitting in the TV area next to an older woman in a hospital bed. As I looked at her, her face began to turn into my Grandmother's. And then she spoke the words, "Peachy Keen." My Grandmother's favorite saying. I was so happy to see my Grandmother I began stroking her arm and saying her name. A nurse told me to stop touching her and to move away from her. I got up and walked away and began praying. I don't remember why the nurse, who seemed very angry, called security but she did. My son was supposed to be coming in to visit me that day. I ignored the nurse and continued down the hall and into my room. The guards rushed in the room and grabbed me. I stiffened my body. The nurse sternly said my name as if she were disciplining me. For a second time I was carried away. I screamed my son's name all the way down the hall. I was put in the isolation room once again. I remember kneeling down in the middle of the room. I could feel the warmth of the spotlight above my head. On my knees I slowly rocked back and forth and repeated these words:

Lord

I stand before you

Just a woman

Waiting for her son

And in his eyes

There will be hope, love, and compassion

For all

2006

The nights were the worst in the second hospitalization. Each night around 3 o' clock, I would get out of bed and walk down the dimly lit corridor to the nurse's station. I would ask the nurses for help. Sometimes they wouldn't even look up at me. It felt like my soul was going to wander in dimly lit halls with no human contact for eternity. This sense of endless emptiness was unbearable. With my head bent, I asked God what I had done, again and again, and again. This went on for many nights. Until this day I remember the anguish. In later years it actually inspired the song on the following page.

A Grave Song

When your spirit leaves you

What's left is a shell

But if the kiss of death has passed you by

You'll be spending some time in hell

CHORUS
Because this can bring a strong man down
Begging to be saved
And the very first time this man prayed
He'd be praying for his grave

CHORUS

Philosophers ask their students

How do we know we're here

But if you've ever been told those walls

Don't speak it all becomes quite clear

CHORUS

Accept the one who guides you

To that barred and sterile place

Cause that someone is your angel

Sent down to kiss your face

CHORUS

If you are a lucky one

And those walls no longer speak

Well that angel is your guardian

His love will make you weak

Only a few entries were made in the 2006 hospitalization along with a sketch that repeats itself 8 years later in the third hospitalization

My father sits across from me

I never knew him

His pain, his fears

His hands shake

He writes poorly

He cannot speak

He remains silent

Unable to connect with....

His daughters, his wife, his son

He must be frightened

But he cannot express

Honest love

Because of scars

He lives with pain

He lives with fear

He is lost and cannot find his way home

2006

Caught in between

The more aware

The more doubt

I have to choose

And accept

And once there

Is no more fear

No more doubts

That sense of control

Will step up on stage

The understanding will become clearer

Everything will be sharp

Whichever path is chosen

Is the right path for the

Between the years 2007 and 2013 I would have a couple of part time jobs and also be put on disability. Again, there were no entries during... what I call, more flat line years.

JOURNAL THREE

The third hospitalization would prove to be one of immeasurable suffering. Not only was there the awareness of the dark side but of the results. I actually felt the fear, grief, and pain of everybody: a woman that leapt to her death in 911, Dr. Petit losing his entire family, the shootings at Sandy Hook. I could hardly breathe. The night before I went to the hospital I made a conscious decision to choose love and said the words out loud in my kitchen several times. I believe God heard me.

Once brought up to the floor. Again, I found myself on my knees praying in the moonlight coming through a large window at the end of the hallway. As I prayed preparing to go to the next life, two nurses stood above me. They asked me to get up off the floor because I was making the other patients nervous. I didn't respond. I heard the footsteps of the guards coming. They picked me up and began dragging me down the hall. Later I noticed that my arms were all bruised around the armpits. As they carried me off I screamed, "Oh no, this is happening again. Please don't bring me back there!" I did not want to go back to earth. Then I heard the guards say, "Here it comes." and I felt a huge deep rush of air enter into my body. This time I was put on a bed that was framed in oak wood. I don't remember them giving me a shot. I just remember being thrown on the bed. They left and I lay in the darkened room. I remember it felt like something beyond my existence was taking place, something very significant. I began to relive all the physical pain I've experienced throughout my life. My legs squirmed as I relived being in full blown labor with my son while being sent through a CAT scan machine. I think I was in this room for 3 nights and 2 days. I ate my meals on the edge of the hard oak frame. It wasn't very comfortable. I felt as though I were a prisoner. I was emotionally and physically broken. The nurse kept telling me, "Keep calm."

The following journal entries seemed to write themselves. As if God was working through me.

Took place on Saturday November 1, 2014 in the ER Written on the 4th

Felt severe anguish. I was up the night before, remained calm. We waited in the ER for a long time. My pain grew more and more. I said to the nurse, "If I were bleeding you would use a tourniquet, I'm bleeding here!" Adam and Richard left and I was alone. I got down on my knees and begged for mercy. I cried, "I choose God's love, I choose God's love!" Adam and Richard entered back into the room and helped me onto the bed. Still I am uncertain and weak as a kitten. They adjust the bed for me to sit upright. The pain begins once more. Adam asked Richard to leave the room. Adam then tells me to touch the blanket and to focus on something on the ceiling and I do. Adam then holds on to my left arm and Richard reenters the room and takes my right arm. I feared that they would rape me along with other strange men. I continue to focus, trying to clear all thoughts and when my mind was empty the explosion of pure joy and peace came over me. I looked into both their eyes. They were the eyes of angels. This beauty cannot be described by words or compared to anything earthbound. The experience lasted briefly.

Tuesday November 4, 2014

Technology is moving us farther and farther away from what it means to be human.

Wednesday November 5, 2014

Life is a moment. We're here. We're gone. If you can grasp that moment, even for just a second, and choose love, you're life has been well spent.

Words written by men should inspire other men. We need to help one another. These men are God's helper's don't revere them. God is the true poet.

No need to seek validation. God loves you. That's all the validation you need. If you truly feel this, it will empower your soul. You will never go hungry.

Best lessons learned are through self-discovery.

Bask in the light from your flickering candle.

It's not real the angel told me. Because men being buried alive in women's love holes is too cruel for the one's seeking integrity.

Wednesday November 5, 2014

I look into the beautiful eyes of an old man who claims to be Roberto Jesus. I hope he can give me one small miracle and speak the truth without me having to move my lips to ask.

I see so many familiar faces. Faces I've seen throughout the ages. All their fears come to me. I read psalm 115 over and over.

What does it mean to fear the Lord........when a man is broken, as broken as a man can be and even past that. Your soul is hemorrhaging on the cold white floor and you're mopping the blood up with your pounding heart. As you plea and beg for mercy, testifying to his love, no matter what, your hands are clenched, your knuckles white and finally a sense of calm overcomes you. You think you've been saved only to repeat this act again and again. You fear the Lord will punish you for eternity. If you accept this, trusting God will save you at some point, that's what fearing God means. You fear him, trust him, you have a faith so strong it can cause a tidal wave. You drown in his love. And as you're kicking and splashing and gasping for air, finally you touch bottom and then fall on the white sandy shores of heaven. And the sun warms your exhausted body.

Let me know Lord if you want me to take anyone else's hand through this glimmer of light you've given me.

Where do I take a seat?

Wednesday November 5, 2014

I must have been raped many times, yet I don't partake. I feel the sinner/saint's pain.

Sometimes I wish I could disappear

Eventually I'm hoping I can write my own prescriptions

Sometimes it feels like I'm fighting for salvation - my families and anyone else who wants to come along.

Nothingness

Starkness is uncomfortable

So is total darkness

You have 'nothing' to fear

The smallest flickering flame can give you hope

Accepting hope is humbling because it comes from

The other side of the universe

Your darkest fears are those you cannot speak.

I have to have faith in me.

Friday November 7, 2014

I am the creator of this make believe world I have created in my mind. It is not real but the Lord's love is. So I wait.......for the perfect stolen moment.

Through my delusions I experienced, which were not real and in my head, two angels of God came to me. And this I know to be the truth. God loves us and there is salvation for those that don't turn away as frightful and painful as it may seem. I know because I went to a very dark place and fell softly into God's arms.

There are no evil people just tormented souls that suffer unbearably. They need to be saved. They need our love. They need to be treated.

Listening to Eva Cassidy's 'Somewhere over the Rainbow' I've been home all along.

Saturday November 8, 2014

I've gone through time, ending with the beginning. I bit into the apple but I did not chew and swallow.

I sneezed loudly but no one said God bless you.

I'm having a de ja vu as I write this:

Honestly, this pain is greater than any person could withstand. It truly feels the weight of the world is on my shoulders. And the only comfort I need is a cup of warm sweet tea, but when I ask for this I'm given 2 cups of chilled cranberry juice.

I'm listening to 'Follow Me' by Uncle Cracker and an older woman afflicted and trying to keep it together lashes out physically towards a young attractive nurse. The nurse has a minor injury. She'll be fine. Who now has gone to see how the other woman is. Her injury is worse. My skin feels like a cat's fur standing on end.

Sunday November 9, 2014

We're in the longest running show on Broadway, the perfect tragic comedy. We are all the court jesters. The one's who don't know this suffer terribly. Have mercy on us all.

Bless the men on earth. They feel shameful. They carry the weight of the world on their broken backs. Bless the women who truly love them for knowing this and loving them with all their hearts.

The enlightened feel love. All our bodies are beautiful. We are all the same yet all very different. We need to stop despising ourselves. You must have boundaries when living on earth, when you are reborn, you are set free. The fences are invisible. You know where to stop.

I came to learn about love from a hospital bed on the psych ward at Danbury Hospital 7 West.

Monday November 10, 2014

Each and every one of us is capable of having the love of God inside of us.

When you can accept your place in the grand scheme of things you will find peace. Have a seat and just be. Choose love when it hurts the most. You have more than you realize as far as fate goes.... one moment at a time.

You will have salvation if you speak the truth and actually practice it.

Warm someone's heart with a gentle smile.

Great comfort comes from a child's prayer....Now you lay me down to sleep. Pray to God my soul you'll keep.

There is no plagiarism just inspiration expressed uniquely.

Learn from other people's past to guide you through your destiny.

We are all in this together.

"Carpe diem"

Tuesday November 11, 2014

As I write this I can see the words without wearing my glasses. I've been temporarily blind. It's almost crystal clear. There is no hysteria. I have that familiar sensation of inner calm. I practice stoicism....logic.

I so desperately wanted to return to my old life. I am questioning that now.

I hope the distractions of the day don't wash away my calm.

He comes to me with awareness and insight.

You come to me with wisdom. I hear no voices. I see no visions. There are only moments of clarity.

I fear to get to that place where my angels saved me I will have to feel great pain again. This thought is paralyzing. I'm hoping just washing away the fear and pain will be enough.

Again I am reminded about the need to be validated and how it truly is unnecessary in order to find true happiness.

Here are some samples of art that was done during art therapy

The instruction was to make a random shape without taking the marker off the paper. Then find images and render them.

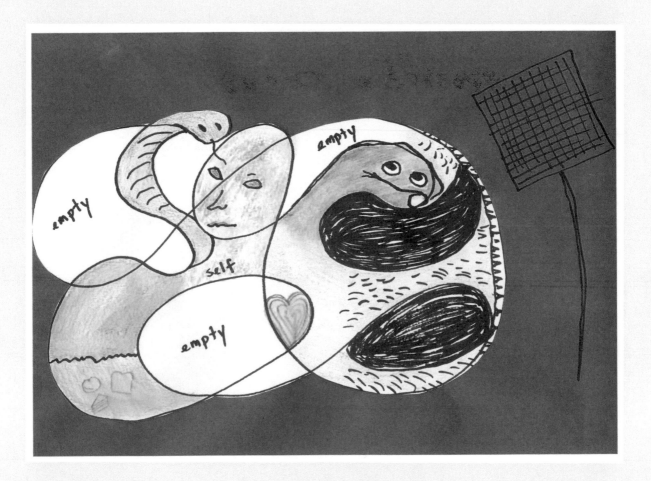

The following is the cover to a card that was done on scratch board.

I addressed it to everyone with the inside reading:

Remember to be in the moment.

Follow your heart.

Be there.

Be.

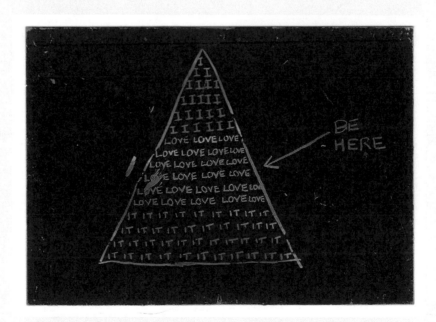

Three months after the hospital, while at home, I began to write in the journal again.

February 3, 2015

Disclaimer: I do not mean all women must bear children to have a purpose or that gay men and women are not worthy. We are all beautiful children of God.

You've heard the phrase - ignorance is bliss. I believe truth is bliss. When you discover the pure truth, a sense of understanding and compassion warms your soul, you've found peace. The struggle we're all faced with manifests itself through all our fears, we become helpless, like small children. The instinct to reproduce and survive, battles our ability to reason. The animal part of us gives us great pain. The reasoning side seeks out love. As humans we need to express ourselves in all forms: art, music, sports, architecture-practically everything we do expresses our attempt to cope or celebrate life. God created man and man needed a companion so he made woman. God also gave us free will and then we made a mistake. He forgives us for that. Man may need woman to continue the human race, but women have a job to, to bare his children and let him know he is exactly what he is suppose to be and the fact that he loves her gives him the dignity of a King.

The real human instinct is to trust. There will be fear, there will be pain, but having faith in love is where the truth lives. Love is energy. The energy of love grows stronger with another person. It starts between a man and a woman. This is why our world rotates. It's a simple science. Spiritually there are no mathematical equations. It's abstract and perfect at the same time. The only symbol we need. I know this is just my interpretation, but if this is what I need to believe, to find serenity for my earthly existence, then I embrace my beliefs.

February 3, 2015

We have seasons because nature keeps getting a second chance. I've been giving a second chance. It feels as though I suffered, died, and went through the gates of heaven, only to be put back in my body to share this experience. At first I thought they were the eyes of Angels but now I know that through my son's eyes I saw Jesus and through my husband's eyes God! Trumpets sound beautiful in heaven. I was astonished! You can say this is a chemical imbalance but it's the imbalance that levels the scales, the weight is the same on either side making the physicality weightless. Simple physics explains our selves. Because a vacuum is created, the first door you go through won't close securely until the next door is opened, only then will the first door close tightly. In order to find closure of your past you need to open up your future. Walk through a new beginning. Like the seasons.

February 4, 2015

How to get to Heaven for dummies

This is not an insult. All our senses need to stop. Our mind becomes still. Once we are still we transcend into euphoria. The sheer excitement of this state will bring us pure joy. You may giggle. Jesus is on your left. God will be on your right. The joy will begin to come in frequencies, like waves and then begin to vibrate. The vibrating becomes intense. At this point I was put back in my body. I can only assume that we explode into stars and then ascend into the heavens. We were made after God's likeness so I believe we'll have faces and bodies but we will be as one. There will be a sense of wholeness.... omnipresence.

My calculator went berserk today then stopped on this number:
.0002571.

February 5, 2015

The key turns slowly as I write. As humans we question everything, our existence, our purpose, the stars, and the galaxy. We've traveled to the moon, the depths of the ocean. My calmness pushes my pen to move. We want to move mountains. When God is in our hearts not only is there room for everybody but the awareness of the infinite truth can build the mountains. Inner peace is expansive. It stretches as far as our imaginations do. Time travel is a human concept. In the spiritual world the measurement of time doesn't exist. As a human you can understand this by removing time from the equation. Finding a starting place is the hardest part. Once you know where to begin, don't be confined, be totally aware of your movements in your space, dressing, brushing your hair, driving your car, keeping your movements mindful, don't let anything become an obstacle.

When you find how you are suppose to contribute to mankind. It will firmly but gently take hold. The driving force will be love. Pray to God for courage so you can carry out what it is he wants you to do.

February 5, 2015

Mitosis and Meiosis

I was watching a rudimentary demonstration on you tube about Mitosis. The chromosomes were represented by beads on strings. Maybe if scientists study Mitosis and Meiosis from a different perspective it would answer a lot of their questions. Has it been literally under their nose the whole time? Instead of using science to explain our existence and the universe, apply God to explain our science.

The transistor is a very simple, small, basic component. But look what it can do. The wheel was probably the most important invention of man, it allowed us to move. Movement is the source of everything, especially when it vibrates.

In the end our preoccupations in life are what we've known all along. And then we begin.

I am inspired by Einstein.

$E mc^2 = 1$

Every man cares to equal one

Again I am reminded. Use God to explain science, not the other way around.

The harmony of our physicality and spirituality will give us serenity.

The Arts and Sciences reveal our selves.

February 7, 2015

Some of us are ships. Some of us are rafts. We are all capable of floating in the same ocean. While the mass is irrelevant, the displacement becomes relevant. The earth is made up of 70 % water, as infants so are we. The unborn child grows in embryonic fluid in order to sustain life. Water is the important element. The surface of water is where gravity meets buoyancy. It's a flat line that sometimes has waves.

February 13, 2015

My alternate world

My first world consisted of experiences, (good and bad), and how I expressed myself. In this world I was quiet for most of it. I spoke and moved cautiously, not wanting to disrupt the peace I so desperately desired. I was affected by negative forces, at times it was excruciating. My spirituality had gone into a tail spin.

One day I came out of the grocery store, stopped for a moment, looked around at the busy parking lot and asked myself, "What is this world?" (Talking Heads song comes to mind) My new world is the opposite of the first. It's different because my perception has changed. Having an understanding of humanity has giving me new insights. I move with a sense of peace and compassion. People behave certain ways because of frustration and misunderstanding. Everything said and done means something. So called mindless yet focused behaviors that involve the restoration or maintenance of order, actually rest our minds. Gardening has been one of my saving graces.

February 13, 2015

My background in graphic design has giving me an edge on the psychology behind visual representation. The goal was to make a connection with a targeted demographic by using two dimensional means. I always liked embossed designs, probably because they appeared three dimensional. What is one dimension? I'm learning the right question is more important than the answer, because if it's right, you already have your answer.

The rhythm of the heart can be monitored. When it flat lines it becomes one dimension, which is all things. There is no need for perception because it just is.

Being human hinders this way of viewing eternal life. Our bodies and everything in our world can sometimes overwhelm us because we have to survive as a species. This is where religion plays an important role in mankind's existence. God wraps you up in a warm blanket on a cold day and gives you toast and tea if you're not feeling well.

Small gestures can give great comfort.

February 14, 2015

When I reflect on my experiences, it feels as though I died many times, with the final death being a sacrificial one. One night in the hospital I remember a sound that had a rhythm, like a whip might have whipping somebody. It felt with each psychological lashing, I would flinch and brace my body. The last lashing paralyzed my body. I thought I would have to sacrifice my daughter. I was stricken with grief and fell out of bed to the floor. As my head went to hit the floor, I felt a pair of arms softly cradle the back of my neck and gently guide me onto the hard surface. Two nurses came rushing into the room. They seemed very concerned that I could not move or speak. They tried to get me to respond by rubbing my neck and chest with their knuckles. It felt uncomfortable but I would not react. Finally, I spoke: "I only answer to God." One of the nurses said to me, "God helps those that help themselves." With these words, I managed to get up on my knees and get back into bed. I've found myself on my knees many times, either praying, waiting to go onward to the next life, or begging for mercy.

It's humbling how small I am.

February 20, 2015

As I become accustomed to my body again, I realize I need to take care of my body and make it strong. I've already seen how resilient my spirit can be. My vessel needs to become just as resilient. My daughter, who is a personal trainer, has been the driving force behind my new quest for improvement. My son will also, be an inspiration. He's capable of amazing things. I beam with pride when I realize just how great both my kids are. Each contributes in their own unique way. Lately, I've been engaging in life. When there's an opportunity to make someone smile or feel good, I take it. This is very fulfilling for me. Small acts of kindness can mean a difference in someone's life.

Lent has begun, and for the first time as a Catholic, it has taken on a new meaning because now I finally understand the significance. It's personal. I just hope I don't breakdown on Good Friday. I'll have to remember to bring a lot of tissues.

February 21, 2015

Practicing Meditation

I need to be alone, sitting near the pellet stove, where I can see and hear the flame is helpful. First I quietly talk to God, asking for strength and guidance. Then I confess my shortcomings. I tell him I want to be close to him. This is our time. Imagine how great his love is, to find time for us all. After my talk, I close my eyes, aware of the flame; I start to feel the energy surge. It seems to resonate in my chest and remain there. Sometimes I am aware of someone else's suffering, that's when the surge is strongest. This is when I feel closest to God. At times the fire makes a groaning sound, as if it's going to speak. This is a new sound me and my family have noticed this winter. I'd like to think that He is present when this occurs. It hasn't been apparent lately. I think I need to stay in touch with prayer more.

February 26, 2015

What is greatness? Is it the?

March 7, 2015

God's love is immense; it is infinite and spans the universe. Each and every one of us is individual universes - waiting to be discovered - by ourselves - not alone but through God.

March 18, 2015

We are all recovering, some from mental illness, disease, afflictions, grief, addictions. We look for medicine to cure our ailments. We ache for peace and tranquility, an existence without pain and constant struggle. Each day we face our own version of war. We all process reality differently, the battles are personal. We can learn from a person or group of people who achieve success spiritually, despite the difficult obstacles. There is inspiration in many people, young and old alike.

Become selfless with no ego.

Unspoken love is best.

Emanate.

June 4, 2015

This is not an entry I took from my journal. I'm just writing it as I type. Lately, the greatest comfort I've been finding has been through kindness I've shown complete strangers, people who reveal themselves to me. I try to show them compassion and give them hope with kind words. Somehow it relieves the ache of my own heart of what I believe to be a failing marriage. I could be faced with losing the home I raised my children in, everything that gave me peace at one time - the gardens, the rooms and hallways, I guess it's everything all around me. The one thing missing is Richard's real love. He has completely shut me out and wants to settle for a marriage of convenience. If he's done with me, I wish he would just let me go. I'll be ok. It won't be easy, but now that I have faith, I won't crumble. I've been through much worse.

I know I am partly to blame. Since, I found God in November; the negative forces have been relentless. Each day I draw my sword to fight a battle of torment that the people around me have no idea I'm fighting. All they see is an irrational person lashing out. Sometimes the desperation brings me to tears. Fighting a war alone is not easy.

Staying connected is important. Doing volunteer work and being with people who are less fortunate helps me to focus on helping others and not suffocating myself in my own trials. I also feel a very strong connection to people now. I see myself in many people, people of all races and gender. I attend church regularly and have been learning the rosary. At our church there's a white bench that sits in front of a statue of Mary. I've been sitting there lately saying the rosary. Sometimes I raise my head and close my eyes as I pray. The light comes through my eyelids and I bask in the warmth that surrounds me.

I don't think I should make this a conclusion. It's really a new beginning, with new discoveries and experiences that lie ahead. I'm a little uncertain because the unknown can be scary. I have to keep my thoughts positive and persevere and keep asking myself, "What would Jesus do?"

Printed in the United States
By Bookmasters